Kristin,
Seek the mac
in each moment
wear the lipstick!

Xo,
Anna

MY LIPSTICK JOURNEY THROUGH CANCER

On Faith and Finding the Right Shade

ANNA M. WARNER-MAYES

ISBN: 978-1-7169-3638-8 (sc)
ISBN: 978-1-7169-3637-1 (e)

Library of Congress Control Number: 2020909151

First published by AuthorHouse Publishing 1/31/2011

ISBN: 978-1-4567-3002-4 (eBook)
ISBN: 978-1-4567-3003-1 (Soft Cover)

Lulu Publishing Services rev. date: 05/19/2020

Cover design by The Crimson Fox
Photo by Kat Stevenson

CONTENTS

PREFACE

I was a teenager in the decade of big hair and fun music. Post Cheryl Tiegs and Farrah Fawcett, people like Christy Brinkley graced the cover of *Sports Illustrated*. I grew up in a time when bigger hair but thinner lips were "in," so I was ashamed of my big lips. Bringing attention to them with lipstick was out of the question. It wasn't until after I finished college that fuller lips became a style obsession, with actresses like Angelina Jolie and models like Claudia Schiffer proudly highlighting their exotic features and luscious lips. The trend has only continued, and now, women are still getting cosmetic lip procedures to make their lips fuller.

After I got my first "real" job post college and took on the responsibilities of adulthood (bills, taxes, and the like), I'd find myself at the mall browsing the shops. But I feared spending my hard-earned money on anything. I would compromise with myself. *I can buy lipstick. It's cheaper than shoes.* That thought ran through my mind again and again. That's when the addiction began.

Fast-forward to today—I am a lipstick fanatic. I have tried just about every brand from nearly every drugstore and department store. I love that lipstick can match your clothes or your shoes, and I love how lip color has the power to transform your face and your mood or your outlook for the day. A perfect red can give you confidence, a pale pink can make you feel hopeful, and a coral can bring you to the tropics.

In my quest for the perfect shade, texture, consistency, and staying power, I have collected buckets of lipstick. Over the years, the price of lipstick has increased in both department stores and drugstores. Today, certain lipsticks cost more than shoes, so my whole theory on lipstick being the less expensive option at the mall is no longer valid. I refuse to throw any of them out, so I have given them away to girlfriends and to my mom. I don't think my mother has had to purchase lipstick in over twenty years.

When I was first diagnosed with cancer, I found myself at lipstick counters trying on various shades of lipsticks, trying to improve my mood, explain it, or just disguise myself from the reality of my diagnosis. Lipstick and the ladies at the counters became my therapy. I had no family history of any kind of cancer. I had supposedly the "best" and "easiest" type of cancer with a high cure rate, but my story wasn't destined to be that simple.

My journey has taken many turns and, along with that, many lipstick hunting expeditions. Faith was my rock and my cornerstone, but lipstick became the "closed-captioning" of everything happening internally in my heart and my mind after my diagnosis. I invite you to join me on my lipstick journey through cancer—one step, one day, and one color at a time.

1

The Diagnosis

At thirty-eight, I had three young kids; worked a full-time job as a pharmaceutical sales rep; and was singing at church, weddings, and as a guest at local events. I was in my prime—rushing from activity to activity, while pursing my real passion of singing. Life was rushing by, and in fall 2007, when I developed a persistent sore throat, I kept on, masking the ache with cough drops and cough syrup. It wasn't until I noticed slight changes to my singing voice that I made a trip to the doctor, which led to my first round of antibiotics, along with a recommendation to start taking allergy medicine. In Michigan, the fall allergy season was kicking in, so it seemed fitting. But as time moved on, my throat stayed sore and then ached in the evenings after a full day of working and singing. The holidays approached, and I was singing more and more. After a second round of antibiotics, my voice still didn't have the same stamina it usually did. I couldn't reach some of the higher notes, and after singing just a few songs, my throat ached so badly that even swallowing hurt.

On a night between Christmas and New Year, after singing at an event, I was massaging my neck while waiting in the car for pizza delivery. That's when I felt a lump. I guessed that it was probably swollen lymph nodes from allergies or that sore throat that I just couldn't kick out of my system. I was gently feeling around my neck area, when I noticed another lump near my shoulder. You know the indentation behind your clavicle? That's where the lump was, and it was not small. Sitting in the silent darkness of my car, I still believed I had swollen lymph nodes from some infection my body was trying to fight, but finding that second lump made me a little nervous. I picked up the pizza and headed home, where my five-, seven-, and ten-year-old awaited me (and the pizza).

"Can you feel these lumps?" I said to my husband, a doctor, as the kids started to fill their plates with slices.

"They just seem like swollen lymph nodes. They should go away on their own," he said.

Though I considered him my at-home medical expert—since he had his own occupational health practice—and should have been satisfied with this answer, I wasn't. The ongoing soreness had made changes to my voice, and I had already gone through two rounds of antibiotics.

"I'll be calling a doctor to set up an appointment," I said, but wasn't sure which kind— family practice or ENT (ear, nose, throat doctor)—so I asked my husband.

"Well, family practice will give you an antibiotic, and an ENT will want to cut because they're surgeons. I think you should just wait it out," he said.

But I had already *waited it out.* So ignoring his expert advice, I went ahead and scheduled my appointment with an ENT for the day following the New Year.

On the morning of January 2, I went to the ENT appointment by myself. When the physician walked in, I described the sore throat I had endured over the past few months and told him about my vocal fatigue in singing and speaking.

He stood silently while I spoke and then said, "Okay. I'd like to scope your throat."

I didn't know what that meant, but I have a terrible gag reflex, and scoping my throat did not sound pleasant. You know those wooden sticks doctors put in your mouth to hold your tongue down while they look? I gag just thinking about it, so I knew scoping would not be fun.

Within a few minutes, the doctor was holding what looked to me like a long metal pipe cleaner. He said it was going to somehow reach the back of my throat so he could peek.

No. Way.

I steadied my breath, fearing the pain and the gagging, but the need for answers calmed me down enough for him to press the instrument down my throat (counting down from ten also helped). When he was finished, he set the scope in a liquid-filled container to sterilize it. Then he took his gloves off and said, "I see nothing unusual, so I believe you have thyroid cancer. You're the right age, you're female, and that lump is in the right spot. We'll help you schedule an ultrasound and biopsy to confirm."

Silence filled me and the small, white, sterile room. Just

me and a stranger in a blue dress shirt, me sitting in my work clothes on a hard exam table.

Then he said, "Don't worry. Thyroid cancer is the best cancer to have. I take out your thyroid, you drink radioactive iodine, and you're done. Highly curable."

He left the room, and then I left the room. At checkout, I was given the order for the ultrasound and blood work, along with a list of places I could go for the ultrasound appointment. I had cancer. But it was an *easy* cancer. I was scared, yet somewhat comforted.

The time between the doctor's office and getting home to tell my husband is a little fuzzy. I know I did one thing for sure. I looked for the nearest place with Wi-Fi, got on my computer, and googled thyroid cancer. It did sound easy, and it did sound curable. I was going to be okay.

The very next day, I went to get blood work and an ultrasound, and immediately after that, I found myself at the Macy's Bobbi Brown counter trying on lipsticks, talking to Diane.

Diane was a makeup artist for Bobbi Brown, and she split her time between Macy's and Nordstrom. She was about fifteen years older than me, was married, and had a son in the military. She herself was a petite beauty with short blond hair and a feisty attitude. What I loved about Diane was that she was always brutally honest (both with makeup and with life advice), and she always pushed me to try new things. She is one of those women who wore her heart on her sleeve and always said what was on her mind.

The minute Diane saw my face, she knew something was

wrong. I told her my story from feeling the lump to that day's ultrasound. She walked around the counter and hugged me, encouraged me, and then found me a beautiful soft brown / plum colored lipstick.

"You look beautiful," she said. "The color perks you up."

Twenty-two dollars was cheap therapy, wasn't it?

~

Lipstick: *Fig.* A brownish, plum, pink color that matches everything. The perfect *your lips but better* color. Wearing it made me feel natural but with a little bit of color. I wasn't standing out, but I wasn't disappearing either. Just me trying to stay afloat and telling the world, *I'm still here … but barely.*

~

Two days after my neck ultrasound, I was at the hospital for an ultrasound-guided fine-needle biopsy. And by the end of that day, I was scheduling my first surgery.

My cancer journey had begun.

Now What?

I have cancer.

I repeated the phrase over and over again, continually followed the words with, *But it's the easy kind.*

I researched thyroid cancer more in depth and found that about two hundred thousand people were diagnosed every year (although that number has been increasing dramatically over the years). I learned that mostly women were diagnosed and that the overall five-year survival rate was 98 percent. So the doctor and everyone who had called, texted, or emailed who somehow knew someone who'd had thyroid cancer were right—it was the "easy" cancer.

I read that after a full thyroidectomy (removal of the thyroid), patients would drink a radiation cocktail called radioactive iodine and that would be it—98 percent survival. I would be on thyroid medication for life (which has its own challenges), but I would be done. Cancer would be gone.

The diagnosis was still shocking, of course, but the words *easy* and *best* outweighed the word *cancer* and put my mind at ease. I didn't ask God, *Why me?* because, Why not me? I wasn't any more special than anyone else. Everyone around me had something big or small they were dealing with. Cancer was my "thing," but we shouldn't compare "things," right? Comparison robs us of daily joys, and what may be small to you could be a gargantuan obstacle to someone else and his or her life situation. So why not me?

My first call wasn't to a family member or even to my husband. I called one of my best friends and coworkers, Michelle.

"I have cancer," I told her.

Michelle: "What? Oh my gosh. What now?"

"No big deal. It's the easy kind," I said. "They take out my thyroid, I drink radiation, and I'm done. I should be back to work within a couple of weeks."

"I think you might be in denial."

"Nope. For real. It's just that easy. Thyroid cancer is the best one to have," I said. Denial or not, I convinced myself it was no big deal. I would be back at work in a week or two because I was strong, and this was easy.

I headed to my parents' house and told my mom and dad. "Well, it's cancer."

Immediately, my mother fell to the floor in the middle of her kitchen and started crying. "How can that be? We have no cancer in our family."

My dad, who is always calm and steady (although I believe it's because he holds things inside like me) was calmer. His response: "Okay. It's okay. What happens next?"

My mom is a strong woman. She and my dad emigrated

from the Philippines when I was two years old without family or knowing anyone. They both had college degrees and great jobs in the Philippines but wanted to live the American dream. My dad, the accountant, and my mom, the social worker, had both worked hard so their kids could have a better life with more freedoms and opportunities. Now, their firstborn was telling them she had cancer. I get it. She was devastated and understandably so. Being a mother myself, I know the feeling of wanting to protect your children and the need to take away their hurts. Telling your mom you have cancer is difficult, but being a mother hearing the news from your child is probably ten times worse.

"I guess I'm the first then. Don't worry. This one's simple. They take it out, I drink radiation, and I'm done. No big deal."

When I told my husband I had thyroid cancer, he said, "Oh good. That's easy. You'll be fine. Everyone survives that one." That of course was the typical statement I heard from many people throughout this process—easy cancer, highly treatable, high survival rate.

⁓

Surgery was scheduled for Thursday, January 31, three days before Super Bowl Sunday. Tom Brady was playing—Patriots versus Giants. This was the year my husband had chosen Tom Brady as his quarterback for his fantasy football league, so he was super excited, and on top of that, a friend had given him an extra ticket to the game in Phoenix.

When I told my husband about the appointment, he was a little upset. His plans for attending the Superbowl had obviously been thwarted by his wife's cancer. He asked if there was any possibility of any other surgery date, but unfortunately, this was the first available and I wanted the cancer out ASAP. I'm not a football superfan, so I had no idea when the Superbowl was, but it didn't matter because my focus was to get the cancer out. There would be future Superbowls, and Tom Brady had lots of time and many seasons still to be a superstar quarterback (obviously). So this one, he had to miss.

Instead of being consoled by my husband, I went to visit Catherine. Catherine mainly worked for Estee Lauder, but she bopped around to all the counters at my local Nordstrom. Super petite, long brown hair, and younger than me by about ten years, Catherine always had a smile on her face and a story to tell. She knew lots of people and lots *about* people. Outside of the makeup counters, Catherine was ultra involved in community theater and actually knew my baby brother from the theater world. She knew who I was because of my singing days. She also was a local singer who sang in a group at a local college, and she was half Filipino. Needless to say, we had *lots* in common.

When I saw her weeks before my surgery, she did a full-face makeover. She told me I should highlight my cheeks and use more eye makeup to look more mysterious. Since makeup rules say you should only highlight one feature (according to all the magazines I've read. from *Glamour* and *Mademoiselle* to *Vogue* and even *Good Housekeeping*) and since my eyes were done, Catherine chose a pale, nude lipstick with a pink undertone.

~

Lipstick: *Nude*. A medium beige that matches your skin. Very few people look great in a nude lip, and if you have light brown skin like me, the wrong nude makes your face look dirty or washed out. If you choose to wear this color, definitely wear more blush and eye makeup.

3

Dark Days

My surgery was more complicated than what the "easy" cancer suggested; it should have been a forty-five-minute procedure. The surgery lasted seven hours, and during the procedure, my right recurrent laryngeal nerve was cut, leaving my right vocal cord permanently paralyzed. I didn't know this when I woke up, but I do have a vivid memory of what I saw before I opened my eyes in that recovery room. I don't know if it was a dream or a vision, but what I saw has never left me. I saw a stage, with a black curtain behind me and a bright light shining in my face. I was overcome with joy and peace while singing the old hymn written by Horatio Spafford, "It Is Well":

> When peace like a river, attendeth my way,
> When sorrows like sea billows roll
> Whatever my lot, thou hast taught me to say
> It is well, it is well, with my soul
> Just before opening my eyes, two nurses spoke.

"That's terrible. Who is here with her?"

"Her parents and her sister are out there."

Sister? I thought. *I don't have a sister.*

I opened my eyes to see the two nurses standing there smiling at me and heard the faint beeping from the monitors I was attached to. I was still groggy but was so excited and thankful to be awake. The surgery was done.

"Hi honey, surgery is over. We have to ask, do you feel safe in your home?" the one nurse asked.

"Yes," I said, thinking that was odd.

"Are you sure? Because there's a man yelling out there who says he's your husband, and we just want to make sure you're okay with seeing him."

"Of course," I said. "It's just his tone of voice. It's regularly loud. He's just worried about me."

His loudness was no surprise to me. He had no control over my situation. I was in recovery. In his mind, the nurses were keeping him from seeing his wife, and therefore, they were in control. Earlier in the day, my parents had brought me to the hospital for the surgery because my husband couldn't leave his clinic unattended. This was the first time he was seeing me in the hospital. His small outburst was part of my "normal" life. He was just showing that he loved me and wanted to protect me.

They glanced at each other and disappeared. When my husband came in, he had tears in his eyes and told me the surgery had gone long and that the prognosis wasn't great. He also told me that my vocal cord would be permanently paralyzed.

I thought he was joking. He told me to look at the clock, and I realized he was serious.

I turned my head slowly and looked. It was seven hours later. At that exact time, I felt overwhelming peace and told him not to worry because all would be okay. I remembered the vision I had seen just before waking up and was absolutely certain that everything would be all right.

I was moved into the ICU after the recovery room because of my compromised breathing. Since my nerve had been cut, the doctors wanted me to be observed that first night. The fear was that my vocal cords would slam shut, and I would not be able to breathe. My parents were there, along with my kids and husband and my friend Michelle from work, who the nurses' thought was my sister. My white sister?

Michelle showed up a half an hour after the surgery began with a gift basket from my coworkers filled with various items to make a hospital stay more bearable. She ended up staying the entire seven-hour duration of my surgery, sitting with my parents. When the doctor came out to speak to them in a private room regarding the seriousness of my case, my mom grabbed Michelle's hand and asked her to come help them understand it all because my husband wasn't there. That's why the nurses thought she was my sister; she never left my parents' side. From that point on, my parents considered her family.

The first night post-surgery, I was lying alone in the dark, the machines beeping, certain that God still had a plan for me. I did not see my doctor after the surgery, so I still had many questions. My mom wanted to stay with me, but my husband wouldn't let her because he thought she'd be in the way of the medical staff. So against her wishes to stay with her child, she left. I was left alone.

Lying there in the darkness, I couldn't help but think. *Stay calm for the kids. What happened today? How bad is it? Where's my doctor to tell me exactly what happened? Don't cry. Stay strong. Is that male nurse really going to be responsible for my bedpan all night?*

My mind wouldn't stop. I kept the television on twenty-four hours to keep me company.

Are the kids okay? Are they being taken cared of? Am I going back to work next week? Should I call my boss tomorrow? What shows are on? What time is it? How many products does QVC have? How am I going to purchase that amazing concealer for nineteen dollars and some change if I'm going to be in this bed all night? Where is my phone? Where is my purse?

Minutes passed. Hours passed. In the darkness, with only the light of the TV and the monitors I was attached to, nauseous from the IVs and pain meds wearing off post-surgery, in and out of sleep, my mind was fully active.

I feared that I would stop breathing in the night. I feared the unknown. With all the questions about the surgery and prognosis swirling in my head, I felt as if I was wearing a blindfold while lost in the woods. I wasn't sure what the next step was going to hold. A short twelve hours earlier I had been prepping for surgery, thinking it was only going to last about forty-five minutes and that I'd be home the next day. Now, here I was in the darkness of an ICU room with just the light and beeping of the machines monitoring my condition, alone. I don't remember how much I cried that night or if I cried at all. I still felt at peace with whatever God had planned, but I had so many questions.

The questions lingered—so many questions.

What happened during the surgery? Why didn't my doctor come talk to me afterward? Where is my doctor? Why am I alone? So, if I have to pee will that male nurse have to see all my junk down below to catch it? Will he see my boobs? Does my breath smell? Did I shave my legs today? When can I go home? What if I do stop breathing? What is God's plan? What if I die tonight?

It was a long, restless night. And yes, that male nurse did have to change my bedpan a couple of times. He was a bigger guy with a scruffy beard, and although smoking was not allowed in or near the hospital, he smelled like cigarettes. He wasn't super gentle, but he was kind and tried to make jokes to keep things lighthearted. I slept on and off, but every time I had to get my vitals checked or "go to the bathroom," there he was without hesitation.

The next morning, a female nurse came in to finish the reports from the night for the next shift.

"Are you Filipino?" she asked while checking my vitals.

"Yes," I replied.

While she wrote in my chart and looked at the IV drip, she asked, "Do you or your mom have any nurse friends who work here at the hospital?" (Filipino nurses equals stereotype.)

I answered, "Probably. Why?"

The nurse grabbed my hand gently and looked me in the

eyes. With a pause and a slight smile, she said, "Last night, there was someone dressed in white who sat at your bedside and prayed for you all night. I'm guessing it was one of your mom's nurse friends."

I half smiled back and shrugged my shoulders and told her I would ask my mom later. She walked to the whiteboard against the wall across my bed and wrote "need-to-know" notes for any medical staff who would come and check on me, asked if I needed anything, and left my room.

When I asked my mom if one of her friends had visited that night, she said no; no one she knew had been in my room. I was in and out of sleep all night, and I hadn't seen anyone in my room. I asked the staff and my friends, but none of them had visited that first night. I never found out who it was. I believe it was an angel, and I knew in my heart I wasn't alone that night. That same night, someone had sent an email to my church asking them to pray for a girl from the vocal team who was in the ICU. I knew, without a doubt, that God was with me.

The days following the surgery were some of the darkest in my life. I was moved to a regular room and stayed there for the next few days. Shortly after I'd changed rooms early the next morning, my doctor finally came to talk to me; this was the first time I'd seen him since before the surgery the previous day. My Paul Simon (Simon and Garfunkel) look-alike doctor anxiously walked in my room with his light blue scrubs on, prepared for another day of surgeries. His face spoke volumes about what had happened during the surgery and what he'd seen. He looked nervous walking toward my bed to talk to me.

I couldn't interpret his demeanor, but he wasn't smiling. *Did he do something wrong? Did he see something bad? Am I dying and he's afraid to tell me?*

Avoiding eye contact and speaking like he had to complete a hundred-page dissertation in five minutes, he first opened my chart and started showing me multiple pictures of the inside of my neck. He was frantically saying, "See? See? That's all tumor. I've never seen anything like it."

Seeing pictures of the cancer inside my neck was something I (a) did not want to see and (b) could not understand. I didn't see the differences in any of the what seemed like hundreds of pictures he tried showing me.

"Do you see all of that tumor?" He was almost shouting.

"I don't know what I'm looking at," I replied.

Looking down and pointing at numerous spots on all the pictures, he was saying, "There and there and there—all of it. There's so much tumor. We couldn't get it all."

What did he just say? He was talking so fast and saying lots of words, but none of them mattered to me. At this point, I just wanted to know two things. How bad is it? And what do I do next?

During the surgery, he had accidentally cut my laryngeal nerve supplying my vocal cord, which left my right vocal cord permanently paralyzed. This, of course, was listed as one of the risks of surgery. So I'd always known in the back of my mind that it could happen. The doctor told me that the cancer was everywhere, which had made the surgery complicated, so he'd had to call two other surgeons in to assist. As he told me all the details of what had happened in the operating room, all I could see was his mouth moving but all I could hear was the hum of the television. Too many words.

I snapped back into reality when he said, "It's bad. It's really bad."

"Bad like the recovery is going to be bad? Like it will take longer than usual? Bad like I'm not going to sing anymore?" This was my response because I couldn't comprehend what he was saying.

He looked at me like I was crazy for asking and then looked me straight in the eyes and, with his eyes wide and frantic, said, "Sing? You're definitely not singing ever again. And no, by bad I mean I'm not sure you're going to make it. What I saw in your neck was bad, aggressive. I've never seen anything like it."

He wasn't warm and fuzzy by any means. He was direct and matter-of-fact, but he had a tinge of nervous in his voice. And with that last statement, he said, "I'll see you in a week in my office after you're discharged. I'm sorry," and walked out of the room.

What was he saying? Was I going to die? This was supposed to be the easy cancer. My initial thoughts were that I didn't care about the singing as long as I lived. I don't know what was worse, sitting alone in the hospital room after he left or seeing my family—my kids—later that morning after having received such devastating news. I went back and forth between feeling numb and crying my eyes out.

When my family finally showed up midmorning, I could barely speak. I was extra nauseous as all of the anesthesia meds the surgical team had fed me during the seven-hour surgery the day before were making their way out of my system through all of my pores. Seeing my young children for the first time after getting the news tore my heart in two. I was both nauseous from all the meds swirling in my body and shattered to pieces looking at my kids. I did not want to cry in front of them, so I kept a smile on my face through gritted teeth.

My husband handled the cancer prognosis a little differently. After visiting that morning, he went straight home with the kids and locked himself in our bedroom. My mother-in-law had flown in from Florida to help at home, and my retired parents were there 24-7, so the kids were well taken cared of. When he finally emerged from the bedroom three hours later, I was told that he headed straight to the basement, got a paintbrush, and started to do touch-up paint all throughout the house. He couldn't fix me, so he tried to fix the flaws with our house. That was how he was.

Throughout that first day post-surgery, I had several visitors—my parents, friends, and coworkers. It was so hard facing all these people who I loved, thinking that my time may be cut short. All of the emotions associated with maybe having to say goodbye and still wondering what exactly was happening were overwhelming. I loved every single person who came into that room. And as more and more people came to see me, I could feel my heart and my insides tearing their way out of my skin. The love and the pain I felt was too much, so by late afternoon, I couldn't face another person.

I buzzed the nurse in and told her through tears, "I can't. It's too much. Please, no more visitors today."

"Okay. I'll make a note of it because we are about to go through shift change," she said, smiling at me with understanding.

She had been in my room to check on me and my vitals several times that day. Every single time she would sit on my bed and ask if I was okay. Every single time I would cry and tell her I didn't know if I was okay and that all I could think of was my kids. She did her best to comfort me, always holding my hand or rubbing my shoulder gently. She would not leave my room until I had calmed down. Nurses and all the caregivers responsible for your comfort and well-being are rock stars.

Me (through tears): "Thank you."

God had a better plan. Just as I was feeling my lowest and during that shift change, the two lead pastors from my church walked into my room. I started weeping immediately. All the fear, exhaustion, and emotion poured out, and the weak facade of strength I had left me. I felt like God had sent them just as I was starting to fall, so that I could feel God's arms catch me and hold me and remind me again that I was going to be okay (in whatever sense that was). They hadn't heard the news of how my surgery had gone, but they'd felt pulled to come see me, especially after the church had received the anonymous email from the hospital.

I raised the head of my bed so I could sit up while they stood at the foot of the bed. Steve, the head pastor of my church, told me the story of how a nurse had emailed the church office the night before asking for a prayer for the girl who sings. Dave, the associate pastor, commented on the books I had on my food tray and spoke about his son, who wanted to be an author because he loved the author of one of the books on my stack. Both had tears in their eyes as they spoke.

After a few short minutes, they moved beside me, one on either side; pulled up chairs; and sat. They had not yet heard the details of the long surgery and the gravity of the prognosis. I shared what I could, with long moments of silence, tears, and sniffling in between. They both sat, leaning in and listening intently since my voice was so soft, not saying a word. After what seemed like hours of me talking (which was probably less than fifteen minutes), I said, "So I don't think I'll be able to sing at the church anymore."

They both moved in at the same time and instinctively grabbed my hands and rested their other hand on my shoulders and started praying. I kept my eyes closed but could not stop the tears. My heart physically hurt as they prayed, and I soaked it all in. They stayed for a while, they prayed with me, and they cried with me. I don't remember all they prayed for, but I slept well that night, knowing that whatever happened next, God would be there, holding my hand.

I don't think I have cried more in a twenty-four-hour period, but I woke up the next morning stronger and with greater resolve to fight. I stayed in the hospital a few more days, with visitors here and there, but my husband and kids never returned because my husband thought it was too hard for the kids. At home, my husband decided to take a sledgehammer to our kitchen, thus beginning the remodel that we had been talking about for months.

Hours of solitude and a bad prognosis led to hours of thinking about life and how dramatically it could change in a day or even in a moment. I thought about how much I wanted to live and to be there for my kids. With cancer, and I suppose with any serious illness, we cling to what's closest to us, including our friends and family. This is a time when love and support reigns, because love and knowing our lives matters is our deepest need. You realize all the things you thought you cared about don't really matter, and you depend on the ones you love to help carry your burden.

My husband of sixteen years decided this was the time to start the remodel of our kitchen. He couldn't control anything that was happening with me, so he chose to start working on the house. He could fix it and not me. So instead of "hanging out" in the hospital doing nothing, he wanted to make the house fresh and new for when I came home. His love language is acts of service, and that is exactly what he was doing for me. Unfortunately, my love language is quality time, and I would've preferred he was with me during one of my darkest moments.

The main thing that kept me fighting was that I did not want my kids to be raised without their mom. That was the flame that lit my fight. I had to fight for my kids.

~

Lipstick: *Black currant / stormy.* A dark, dark lip color. I prefer dark and deep plums and berries. Darker shades are not bad, as long as you keep the color on your eyes and cheeks lighter.

4

Hopeful

Remember when I said my husband took a sledgehammer to the kitchen and finally started the remodel we had talked about? That's what I came home to after spending almost a week in the hospital. Typically (I would think), after a cancer diagnosis, surgery, the ICU, a bad prognosis, and a few days in the hospital, one would come home to rest in a peaceful environment to be able to recover and process. Oh well, peace was not in the cards. The kitchen was a wreck, and I had three young kids running around in the dust alongside broken tiles and drywall. I had no doubts, though, that the finished project would be beautiful.

Our refrigerator was plugged into an outlet in our foyer, and our pantry contents were on a makeshift shelf right next to it. We no longer had our large 1980's microwave, but our oven was still plugged in. Our countertops were gone, along with most of the cabinets, so plates, cups, and silverware were stacked everywhere.

Welcome home, relax, and recover.

Nope.

I came home to three young children, ages five, seven, and ten and was surrounded by chaos from my external environment, which seemed to match the chaos of my internal environment. I was happy to be home, but it was the opposite of peaceful. We had visitors daily. They brought meals, magazines, and gifts for me and sometimes for the kids, which I loved. People came to pray and share stories and to just "be present." It was quite the emotional time, both because of the cancer situation but also to see so many people who cared for me and my family.

I had a strained and soft voice, so I mostly listened or communicated via a small whiteboard and through hand motions. The environment was solemn, but occasionally, there was humor in the chaos. One friend brought a whole Thanksgiving-sized feast, premade and frozen, which only required "heating up in the microwave." All we had was my brother's tiny microwave from college. Each part of that meal took about twenty-five minutes to heat, and we were starving. So as we thawed and ate the mac and cheese, we would stare at the potatoes thawing and then the stuffing. That meal took about two hours to finish.

Despite the circumstances, it was a joyful time seeing everyone. I was grateful that we had meals every day, and we didn't have to figure out how to work around our piecemeal kitchen.

When my husband wasn't at work, he was home and 100 percent focused on the kitchen; the sound of a saw, hammer, sander, or whatever other tool was constant, even through the night. One morning that first week back home, my husband asked if I could grout the kitchen tile since I wasn't doing anything. So of course I did—drain coming out of my chest and all.

Dust was everywhere, so I confined myself to the bedroom or the piano / dining room area, which was on one side of the house. In that area, by our dining table, we set up a small table to hold the tiny microwave, along with our coffee maker. Since this room was near our front door and foyer, we were close to the refrigerator and pantry.

I don't know why my husband chose that exact time to start the kitchen project, but I believe it gave him control of something. He couldn't control or fix my cancer, so he started a project that he could control. I understand it, but all I wanted was for him to hold my hand and tell me everything would be okay and tell me he would be by my side no matter what. He had started a project, and he would finish it. Consequently, at a time I needed him the most, he was focused on getting the kitchen done for me. Again, his love language is acts of service, so this was the way he loved me best.

About a week after coming home from the hospital, I was called to my doctor's office as a follow-up to the surgery and to take out the drain, which was collecting blood and extra liquids in my chest. He came into the room as I sat alone wondering what the pathology report said, and before taking the drain and stitches out, he was smiling.

"How are you feeling?" he asked while grinning.

I was a little taken aback by his wide smile. "Not too bad." *Why is he grinning?*

"The stitches are healing well. Let's take the drain out and then talk about your pathology report."

He told me to take a deep breath and then exhale forcefully. As I exhaled, he swiftly pulled out of my chest what seemed to be a tube that could reach from my chest to my feet. In reality it was probably only about eighteen inches—still long. Relief.

He then continued, "I got your pathology report and guess what? It's still papillary thyroid carcinoma, the most curable kind of thyroid cancer. I thought it would be much worse."

"So, what does that mean for me?" I replied.

"It means I believe the radioactive iodine can get the rest of the cancer, and you'll be done."

"What do you mean?" I asked, feeling a smile starting to spread across my face.

He replied again, "I mean, I think we can get all the cancer with the radioactive iodine, and you'll be fine—cancer free."

He was surprised to get the pathology report because it turned out I still had the most curable form of thyroid cancer, papillary thyroid carcinoma. He told me he'd talked to the radiologist, who'd agreed. They could kill the cancer with the radioactive iodine—easy peasy. I went from being told to "start making arrangements" to having the most curable form of thyroid cancer. It was a mix of joy, relief, exhaustion, release— you name it. I felt as if I had been holding my breath for a week. And finally, I exhaled.

I received so many cards and encouraging emails, some

from people I hadn't spoken to in years and even some from strangers who had heard my story through friends, all of which always brought me to tears. It made me very aware that people paid attention to me and were affected by my actions. If you treat people with kindness and respect, they will remember you. It was overwhelming. Sometimes, it's just one moment or a chance encounter, but even that is enough time to impact someone's life in either a positive or a negative way.

~

Lipstick: *Pink / pink shimmer.* Any variety of pink is like *hope* and *summer* in a tube. Anyone can pull off light pink shimmer. Who doesn't love more hope and a whole lot of summer?

5

Setback

Eleven days after the surgery, I woke up and nothing but air was coming out of my mouth. Since leaving the hospital, I had been able to exert sound, even though I sounded like someone who was straining to talk while having laryngitis. But that morning, the sound was absent. Lying there in bed, I knew something was wrong. Later that morning, as I tried to eat breakfast, I choked on everything. I could not drink liquids or swallow food without choking and violently coughing. Since the kids were already at school and my husband was at work, my mom was at my side daily. I wrote on a notepad for my mom to call the doctor.

I lost all verbal communication. My voice was gone. I was referred to Dr. Adam Rubin, a laryngologist (ENT, vocal cord specialist). Harvard-trained and a former singer/actor himself, he understood how important my voice was to my career as a sales rep and to my passion as a singer. After scoping my throat, he discovered that my left vocal cord was now paralyzed as well, leaving one big open space over my trachea—which was the direct route for food and beverage and explained the choking. He explained that, more than likely, the trauma of the long surgery had caused stress on the vocal fold, so it had stopped working. Of course, that was theoretical. He didn't know why, after eleven days of having a partial voice, it would suddenly stop. He was dumbfounded at my paralysis but did not want to conduct any surgical procedures until the cancer was taken cared of. So we had to wait.

In the months following, I had to point to the food I wanted. I could not go through drive-throughs because no one would hear me, and even inside a fast food restaurant or coffee shop, I had to lean in and whisper my order into someone's ear. I got the nod of understanding from waiters, grocery store clerks, bankers, and everyone thinking that I had laryngitis from a cold. They didn't know that, under the many scarves I wore to cover my neck, there was a three-inch scar across it from surgery. I couldn't speak to my kids, so I had to snap or clap my hands to get their attention. My kids could not hear me say, "I love you," which was heartbreaking. I couldn't sing the special goodnight song to my daughter, which I had done every day of her seven years of life. I wondered if they would ever hear my voice again. You truly don't appreciate health and the miracle of being fully functional until something stops working.

When I could, I went to see Tanita at Macy's. Tanita was a beautiful African American woman who was a floater at the cosmetic counters. Floaters are those ladies who work in the cosmetic area at a department store but are not tied to any particular brand.

I walked straight up to the Bobbi Brown counter where she was working for the day and said, "Things are bad."

With her eyes wide, she responded to me the way she knew I'd like. "Let's find you a lipstick."

Me swiping various colors on my hand until finally finding a color I like.

Tanita, noticing the color I had landed on, said, "You have too many lipsticks that color. Try something else."

I say the thing I think most makeup artists like to hear. "You pick."

They are artists after all.

We went from pink, to red, to brown and I settled on a sheer pearly white gloss. I was feeling dull and depressed, so I thought if my lips looked like they were covered in diamonds, I would shine. But shine doesn't look good on a frown.

Medical Moment: The treatment for papillary thyroid cancer is radioactive iodine or I-131. Basically, patients have to become completely hypothyroid (no meds, sheer exhaustion) and follow a strict low-iodine diet (which is pretty darn difficult to do because just about *everything* you want to eat contains iodine, like chocolate, eggs, seafood, dairy, and just about every packaged product in the grocery store) for about four to six weeks before radiation. Then, when you feel like you can't even lift your legs because you're so hypothyroid, you go to the hospital and drink a small vial of radiation. After you drink it, you have to be in isolation because you're radioactive.

The five weeks between losing my voice and being ready to take the radioactive iodine were long. During the day, the kids were in school and my husband, along with most of my friends, were at work, so I had lots of alone time. I obviously couldn't go back to work because I had no voice, so I was stuck. It wasn't terrible, but a quiet environment lends to lots of introspection and also overthinking.

My days consisted of reading, writing, crying, praying, and playing the piano. I believe I ran through every single possible emotion about every hour—from peace and gratefulness to devastation. At the piano, I would sit and play and hear my voice singing along in my head, which would make me cry because my singing voice was gone. Losing my singing voice hit me hard around this time, and I began the long process of grieving that loss, which would continue for weeks and years to follow.

At the very beginning of my cancer journey, the pastor at my church spoke about hearing from God. He posted a listening prayer in the bulletin, which was basically a prayer including a couple of Bible verses asking God for direction and then being open and available to hear Him. I have always been a little skeptical about actually "hearing" from God. I have wondered whether what I heard was from God or if it was my own internal voice speaking the desires of my heart. I suppose it could be a little of both because doesn't God give you specific gifts and talents and, therefore, the desires you have in your heart? Probably not the selfish desires like a million tubes of lipstick or a Prada bag, but you know what I mean.

During this time of silence and waiting, I read the Bible and prayed a lot. I decided one night to pray the listening prayer after reading a bit and just poured my heart out to God. *God, I'm tired. I'm scared. I can't leave my kids. I love them so much it hurts my heart. Do I love them too much? Is that it? Am I holding onto them too tightly? I want to live. I don't need to sing anymore. I'm sorry if it became too much of my identity and made me forget a little that You gave me my voice. I'm sad that's gone too but I just want to live. Please.*

I've never heard Your audible voice. If I did, would I be able to distinguish between whether it was You or really me and my gut or instinct? How is one to know? I have my desires. You have Yours for me. Are they the same? I'm here. I'm listening. But I don't know what I'm supposed to hear. I'm not sure what I'm listening for, but I'm scared and sad and exhausted. I need You. What is happening? What happened? Is there a lesson? What do You want me to know? Teach me—tell me! I'm Your daughter, right?

I'm begging You for peace. I'm begging You for hope. I'm asking you to please speak to me and somehow make it clear that it's You and not me. I need to know You have not abandoned me. I know You haven't. I need You.

As I sat in silence, I heard the word *trust*. It whispered to me. It whispered to my soul and comforted my heart. I knew it was from God.

He wanted me to trust Him with *His plan*, not mine. My plan was to have no cancer and live happily ever after. It could've been God's plan as well, but this was God letting me know to trust Him and to release control. Despite the roller coaster of emotions, I felt the steady voice of God in my head and my heart, saying, "Trust."

Whatever happened, God was with me and my family. It was unbelievably comforting to release this time into God's hands.

I felt overwhelming peace. It felt as if a weight had been lifted off my shoulders. The tension I was holding in my neck and shoulders dissipated, and I could feel my shoulders and arms relax. I cried as I took deep breaths, releasing the control I thought I had regarding my outcome. I was responsible for my part, and I had to trust God with His. All I could control was how I treated my body in terms of food, rest, and managing stress. I had to trust the doctors I had chosen to do their part too. I had to show up, fight, and live. I had no control of the future and I couldn't change the past, so the word *trust* became my mantra.

When I couldn't sleep from worry, trust God. When I felt like I couldn't breathe because of panic, trust God. When I worried about my kids, trust God. Trust God and love the life I was given—every moment and every breath I was blessed with. Letting go and trusting gave me the peace I longed for and watered the tiny seed of hope that was in my heart.

Not having a voice did not keep me away from my lipstick counters. In the five weeks before radiation, I probably went lipstick hunting twice per week. I was in lipstick overdrive. I looked perfectly healthy besides the bandage on my neck, which was always covered up with a scarf. No one in the public knew there was a storm battling inside of my body and that I could not speak—which was why I would frequent stores like Sephora and Ulta.

At department store makeup counters, you can't just look and try things on. There is always a woman behind the counter asking questions and wanting to help you. At this stage in my journey, I pretty much knew all of those women at every department store near me. At places like Sephora and Ulta, I could browse and play all I wanted, without speaking, and without interruptions. On occasion, someone would ask if I needed help, and with a simple shake of my head, they would go about their business. I had no voice, and I also didn't feel like talking to anyone, so these stores became my hot spots.

6

Quiet, Kids, and Music

Our house was extremely quiet. I had three young kids still in elementary school, ages five, seven, and ten. Normally kids these ages would be running around and rambunctious. But during this period, our house was mostly quiet. The kitchen project was done. One thing about my husband was that, once he started a project, he was fully dedicated to finishing it quickly, even if it meant working all hours of the night. My volume, or lack thereof, dictated the volume of the house. The kids were amazing and adapted well. Even though they were so young, they knew Momma was sick. When they needed me or wanted to tell me something, they would look me straight in the eyes. When I whispered to them, they would whisper back. And when they would not pay attention to me, I would just clap or snap my fingers, and they were at my attention. They knew by my facial expressions how I was feeling and sometimes what I needed. This is the power of the mother-child bond. We were experiencing a time of mutual need—them because they were young, me because I was sick.

The emotion of being a mom with cancer is indescribable. Looking into the eyes of these little creatures you were blessed with and who held pieces of your heart while thinking you may be leaving them? It was too much. My husband and I couldn't decide how much or how little we would tell the kids about the cancer. We told them I was sick and that I had to go to the hospital, but the "C word" was avoided. I would still tuck them in at bedtime and whisper prayers in their ears as they went to bed. All of it made me cry tears they would never see. I had to be strong.

Each child had his or her routine. The oldest would want prayer. My daughter (the middle child) had a song I sang to her every night. My youngest wanted a little of both. But I had no voice, just air—no audible prayers, no song. I only had my whisper, so every night I would stick to the nighttime routine with my kids while my heart was softly breaking. I would hug them like my life depended on it, and when I whispered, "I love you," into their ears, I could feel every last inch of my heart pounding out of my chest and prayed that they could feel my love. My kids were my reason to fight.

During the day in my quiet house, I read a lot. I journaled all my feelings and any positive quotes I'd heard, and I sat at the piano and played songs I had played most of my life. Throughout this whole process post-surgery before radiation, I had been focused on one thing—surviving and getting rid of the cancer in my body. I wanted to be alive for my kids at the end of the day, and my voice was a second thought, but I still missed it.

When my parents first flew to the United States from the Philippines, I was only two years old, but my mother tells me that I sang and danced to everyone the whole twenty-hour flight. She said I would entertain the crowds by singing "Tiny Bubbles" and "Pearly Shells" while doing my best hula dance. Growing up, I took dance and piano lessons, and I loved it all. I was a shy introvert, and music helped me express myself. Different songs penetrated my heart because I could literally feel the music.

When I was eight years old, my parents took me to see the touring production of the musical *Annie*, and I was hooked. I did not know how a young Asian girl was going to transform herself into a redheaded white girl, but I didn't care. I became Annie in my head. I learned every song, made up my own choreography, and repeated my own special production of *Annie* in the family room of my house over and over again. As I got older, I went from learning the songs of *Annie* to belting out those from *Sound of Music, My Fair Lady, Fiddler on the Roof,* and *West Side Story* to singing "Hopelessly Devoted" from *Grease* at the top of my lungs.

In high school, I was a constant soloist in the show choir and taught most of the choreography as well. I was in every school musical, with dance solos and song solos, and eventually starred in the school musical my senior year. When I was sixteen, I sang on a local televised singing competition of mostly adult, semiprofessional singers in the area and was the champion for over six weeks. One of the judges on this singing competition show even compared me to a young Whitney Houston. Whenever stage lights and music turned on, I felt free. I could transform myself into different characters and become the song. The singing, dancing, and musicals continued through college and beyond. In college, I was in musicals and was the opening act for a couple tours coming through.

After college, I was booked for weddings, funerals, commercials, and radio jingles. I even auditioned as the lead for the touring Broadway production of *Miss Saigon*. And out of the 250 girls who auditioned, I was the last one standing. I was handed the music to learn and set to fly to New York that fall. (Life changed, choices were made, and *Miss Saigon* didn't end up being part of the plan.)

I was a worship leader at my church and felt singing was the talent God gave me. Singing, I knew, helped me communicate best. Outside of my career in sales, music and singing had become a huge part of my identity or even my whole identity. I knew it was the one thing I did well. Singing was like breathing to me. It was my passion and my love and something I felt I was made to do.

Now here I was—in my quiet house, no voice, sitting at my piano every day. I grew up learning and perfecting Chopin, Beethoven, and Mozart. But the music I had printed at this point was music that I could play and sing to. My piano bench stored scores to *Les Misérables* and *Miss Saigon*, as well as sheet music to Streisand and, of course, Whitney.

Weeks after the surgery, I sat down at the piano. After the first few notes, I burst into tears. I could *hear* my voice in my head singing the notes and words to the song, but I knew my singing voice was not ever going to be the same. The grief was overwhelming. My voice, which had defined so much of my identity for more than thirty years of my life, was gone.

The tears flowed every time I sat at the piano. I realized that the tears were not only for the loss of my voice, but also for the grief I had after losing trust in my own body. My body had betrayed me, and there was no going back. Sitting at the piano and not being able to sing was the strongest, most in-your-face reminder that I was and would be forever changed.

I had days and days of silence and alone time, but evenings were filled with noise. The kids were home after school, friends were still bringing meals; and, at least until the kitchen project was finished, my husband and his work on it were still loud and obnoxious. My parents were at my house every single day, helping with the kids and helping warm a meal someone had brought. My husband was 100 percent dedicated to his job and to the kitchen. Everyone was doing something, and there I was—desperately seeking out the magic of every moment and trying to be present. On top of the fear of the unknown future, I was struggling with the grief associated with the loss of what I thought was my identity, my music.

I had visitor after visitor bringing meals and gossip about the world happening outside my home. I couldn't really participate in conversation because I had no voice, so I relied mostly on my facial expressions (thank goodness I had been involved in theater). I had the "*no way*" look and the "oh my goodness" look and the "oh that's sad" look, along with the accompanying gasps and hands to cover mouth and rolling of the eyes. Everyone was trying to be "normal" which was where I wanted to be—back to normal.

It was such a strange time of mixed feelings. I had some fear about the upcoming radiation treatment getting the rest of the cancer. I was grieving the loss of my singing voice. And I was trying to maintain a strong face for the kids and for everyone else really. Here's the thing; all the love, help, and support was for me to feel loved, helped, and supported. So, if I hinted at feeling down, then those around me would feel worse. Consequently, I maintained a smile and positive attitude, even though there were definitely difficult days. Beyond all of that, I had an overwhelming sense of gratitude. I was shocked at all the people who showed their support in one way or another, some of whom I hadn't spoken to in years. People are amazing.

Radiation

The day had come. It was almost two months since my surgery, and it was finally time to drink the radiation that would kill the rest of the cancer in my body. It didn't seem like that big of a deal, except for the fact that I still had a lot of cancer left in my neck. Leading up to this day, I was tested to see how much radiation my body could tolerate before it would affect something else in my body negatively. The doctors determined the max dose I could tolerate was 260 millicuries, so they decided I would drink 256 mc, which was a sizeable dose but left space for things to not go sideways.

When I arrived at the hospital, they informed me that, since my radiation dose was so high and because I still had so much bulk tumor in my neck, they wanted me to stay a few extra days in the ICU after radiation. This was news to me. So no overnight bag; no, "I'll see you in a few days," to my kids; and no mental preparation for staying in the same area that I'd been in after my surgery to remove the cancer. This defined how my cancer journey seemed to be going—throwing my hands into the air and rolling with the punches.

At the entrance to the hospital, I said goodbye to my husband and, with just the clothes on my back, was escorted to the ICU room where I would drink the radiation and "live" for the next few days. The first thing I noticed was one of those radioactive hazard signs hanging on the door. Let me remind you, I was in the ICU, so there wasn't exactly any privacy. I had a room with a glass wall because the ICU usually houses the sickest patients, who need to be observed.

Everything in the room was covered in plastic—everything. It was like kids had pulled a prank and wrapped everything in saran wrap. The phone, remote control, every handle, and every faucet—basically everything I could touch or make physical contact with, including the toilet seat—were all wrapped in plastic. After being shown the room, I was handed a plastic bag and told that all the clothes I was wearing would have to be sent home or thrown in the trash and my husband was to drop off new clothes for me when I was discharged.

I was about to be radioactive.

The time came to drink my I-131 radiation. The medical team placed a small lead canister in front of me, slowly unscrewed it, pulled out a small vial of clear liquid, and handed me a straw. As they slowly backed up, they told me to drink all the liquid as soon as they opened it.

The liquid had no flavor, and I was done in about ten seconds. *So that's it? Less than three ounces of liquid is going to kill all the cancer left in my body?*

Afterward, I was in solitary confinement. Food was delivered to my door. The staff would knock and place my food on a rolling tray covered in plastic, and I'd pull my tray in. Everything was disposable. Since I was in the ICU, everything was sterile, and the monitors beeped persistently. I felt totally normal, or I should say *functional*, but I knew that the patients in the rooms surrounding me couldn't even sit up on their own. I was given instructions on how to wash myself and how to dispose of things and how I had to flush three times and wash my hands twice every time I went to the bathroom. I wasn't allowed to shower or leave the room. No one could be in my room for more than five minutes because of radiation exposure. Yet here I was. The radiation was soaking into all of my organs.

Please, cancer, be gone.

Lipstick: *Green.* Not really a lipstick color, although I'm sure you can find it. I chose this color because I received my radiation on March 17, 2008, St. Patrick's Day.

At the end of each day, the physicist would come into my room with her yardstick and Geiger counter to measure how radioactive I was. They had to make sure that I was safe to be in the general public.

I ended up leaving the hospital three days later, and a miracle happened. I could hear a small sound coming from my throat.

My right vocal cord was paralyzed, but I could hear sound. My left vocal cord was starting to function again.

My voice was coming back.

⌇

By April, one month after radiation, my voice had returned. It was weak and breathy, but it was back. I immediately started speech therapy to help strengthen what I had left.

By May, I was back at work, struggling with my voice and breathing but supposedly cancer-free and starting my new "normal." It was both exhilarating to be cancer-free and yet strangely depressing reintegrating into real life again. In just a few short months, I had experienced so many emotions, and now I was back to the same routine with work and kids and friends and home. Cancer, surgery, radiation, or alien abduction and return to earth? I wanted to shake people and tell them that life was awesome and not to waste a single minute. Everything was still the same on the outside, but I had changed a million times over on the inside.

My lipstick trips did not end; they became more energized. I bought reds, deep plums, pinks, and sparkly glosses. I spent hours with my counter girls, pouring over the new colors of the season and anything I hadn't tried yet. It was wonderful therapy being surrounded by people who were being paid to complement me. Different colors transformed my mood and my posture.

Six months later and fully recovered, I started working harder with my voice crew (doctor and speech pathologist). My voice was getting stronger, and my breathing was getting more regulated. My left vocal cord was learning to compensate for my dead right vocal cord, and after a few more months, my speech pathologist said, "I think you will be able to sing again."

My heart had gone from unspeakable grief at the loss of what I thought was my whole identity to exploding with joy. She gave me the name of a voice teacher, and I started working hard to sing again. I was hopeful and so grateful that, after everything, cancer had not taken that very special part of me away.

Almost exactly one year from when I heard a hint of my voice coming back, I was able to sing a song from *Les Misérables* at a concert my voice doctor put on for International Voice Day. I got a standing ovation, and I could not stop crying. It was a miracle. I was cancer-free, and I was singing again. I was no longer a cancer fighter; I was a survivor

That June, I decided to audition for a part in a musical, which my local theater was putting on. I got a part with a few lines and a solo. I was 100 percent back to doing what I loved. Rehearsals began in July and then in August. After getting fitted for costumes, I was scheduled for my final voice evaluation so my laryngologist and speech pathologist could close my case.

It had been seventeen months since my first post-surgery scan—seventeen months of fighting back, gaining health, and coming back to "normal" life. There had been a year of rebuilding my voice and relearning how to sing with just one functioning vocal cord—a year of gaining confidence in my body and myself. In the same week as my final voice evaluation, I had a scheduled routine ultrasound of my neck. I would go in, get a positive response, and return to my day-to-day routine.

It's Back

It was a hot summer day. I had been officially cancer-free for almost fifteen months, and life was moving right along. It was August 6, and I was headed into the routine ultrasound of my neck, with the intention of going to work right afterward. For the past year, I had been doing ultrasounds and bloodwork every few months since being deemed cancer-free. If this ultrasound was clean, then my scans were going to be stretched out to every six months to a year. I was confident I was done with the small cancer blip that had interrupted my life.

I lay on the table in the dim room, all smiles, with my neck propped up slightly. Since I always had scans at the same hospital, I was getting to know the staff. We chatted as the tech prepped me. She put the cool gel on my neck and started to roll the wand around, stopping, clicking, and typing while still chatting with me. At a certain point, she hesitated. Concern flashed over her eyes.

"What is it?" I asked, zero panic in my voice.

"Nothing. Just looking," she responded.

"Okay," I said, but I didn't believe her.

She continued to roll, click, and type. But this time, it was in the same general area of my neck, so I knew she had seen something. The fun smile had faded from her face and now, she appeared laser focused. I could feel my confidence slipping. When she finished, she simply said, "I'll be right back."

I forced a smile.

A few minutes later, the doctor came in and sat at the ultrasound machine. *Just stay strong*, I told myself. *It's fine.* I tried to keep my eyes blank as I stared at the white ceiling, emotionless. More gel on my neck, roll, click, type. On occasion, I would side-glance at the doctor to try to distinguish his facial expressions, but I couldn't tell. Doctors are good at that.

When he finished, he put the wand down and stood over me.

The doctor's first words were, "There's something there."

"Like scar tissue?" I asked.

"No. Like something suspicious," he responded. Suspicious is not a fun word for a cancer fighter.

"Like more cancer?" I felt the shakiness of my voice but tried to remain calm.

"Well, we won't know for sure until after a PET scan."

"So now what?" Still calm.

"We schedule a PET scan."

I literally felt my heart drop into my stomach. I felt sick. He told me I was done and that I could go ahead and change. He would be calling my physician, and I would get a call from the scheduling department for that PET scan. I was numb as I got up and changed out of the hospital gown, back into my *normal* clothes. I don't remember feeling anything until I walked out of the hospital. I'm not even sure how I made it to the exit. I do know that I didn't make it much past the exit doors before I had my breakdown. I stood against the hospital building in the warm air, leaning onto the cold bricks, and cried so hard I couldn't catch my breath.

My cancer was back. It was back in my neck, across a few lymph nodes, and another tumor was resting on a nerve. Devastated couldn't even describe it; my brain hurt, my heart hurt, I felt delirious, and nothing was making sense to me. Fear crept up and surrounded me like the tentacles of an octopus trying to squeeze every bit of hope from every part of me that each tentacle could touch. I could feel every nerve of my body screaming to free itself from the fear of the unknown not just for me, but again, the kids. On top of that, I had sadness seeping from every pore that fear didn't cover. It was a punch to the gut.

After almost fifteen months being cancer-free, I was finally feeling like my life was back to normal. I was working again, singing again, and being an active mom to my kids, but cancer knows no bounds; it has no rules. It came back when I least expected it.

I cried the rest of the afternoon and made several phone calls. I called my boss, my best friends, my husband, and my mom. I didn't know what to do with myself. There were so many questions: What now? Surgery again? Radiation? What?

At some point in the evening, after taking the rest of the day off of work, I started to pray. *God, I'm not sure what You have in store for me and for my family. I will still not ask why because I know You have a plan for me no matter what. I still trust You. Please help me be strong for my babies; shelter them from fear and pain. I pray for peace and calmness. Lead me to the right doctors. I also pray that I keep my voice and for total healing. But again, I trust You and Your plan, whatever that may be. Help me to release control. Fill me with Your peace and give me wisdom and strength. Thank You for my life.*

I knew I still had to trust Him, whatever the outcome. I read a quote that night by an unknown author. "It is not the greatness of my faith that moves mountains, but my faith in the greatness of God." I prayed for that kind of faith. And eventually after awhile, I found peace.

Lipstick. *Brown/beige.* This day, I did not want to talk to people or see my lipstick therapists at the counter. I stopped at the drugstore to buy something invisible. I had been crying all day and wanted to buy a simple color that balanced my red nose and red eyes. A beige lip gloss gave me a finished look. It basically put a shine on the invisible person I wanted to be.

Around this time, the sump pump in our house started backing up. We lived in a twenty-five-year-old house, so we knew this was about the time certain things would need repair. Now that our kitchen was done and put back together, it was time for my husband to start another project. He needed something to occupy his time, especially with my new diagnosis. So with the sump pump acting funny, he went ahead and dug a small hole in our yard to see if a pipe outside was somehow affecting it.

After digging a four-foot hole, he decided to call a specialist. The plumber said that, since our pipes went back into the woods behind our house, the tree roots had punctured and blocked our pipes. He told us that he would have to dig up our yard to look at all the pipes and fix the problem. So, of course, my husband thought this was an opportune time to install a swimming pool. How convenient.

Over the next few days, I mustered enough brain power and stability to research different physicians to handle now a more delicate surgery. They had to go back into my neck, scar tissue and all. I settled on a doctor based on recommendations and scheduled an appointment with him. My friend Michelle came with me to help ask questions and to give her opinion, and after we both agreed he was the one, I scheduled surgery for a month later. I wanted the tumor removed as soon as possible. Being diagnosed with cancer *again* reminded me that life was short. Even though I was almost back to my new normal, this new diagnosis stopped me in my tracks. Still, I was determined to overcome it.

Lip Tip: If you're going with a nude lip and need a little pop, top it with a pink gloss or any gloss with a little sparkle. I always need a pop, even when I'm not wearing an actual color.

9

Quick Turn

I was left with a month to sit and stew before my impending surgery. I obsessed over every possible outcome. The surgery was riskier now because of all the scar tissue and the injury to my laryngeal nerve from the last surgery. August sped by as I tried to keep my head above water. I had to drop out of the musical, which was incredibly sad. My cast mates came together and gave me a small gift and a card with lots of loving words. I didn't know if I would ever be in another show again, so I had to, once again, grieve what was now an even greater possibility— the permanent loss of my singing voice.

By now, even the girl at the local drugstore knew me. What's hard about drugstores is that you can't try any lipstick on. None of the shades I picked worked for me. I even returned to the shades I'd used in college, but they didn't work anymore either. *Does your skin tone change as you grow from a young woman to a more mature woman?* I decided to stick with lip balms and glosses from the drugstore and lipstick from department stores. I had officially become a lipstick snob.

I continued working as usual. But between crying, my mind wandering, thinking about what was truly important in life, and sometimes feeling like I was just losing my mind, I knew I was ineffective. Still, no one, including my boss, said anything. My family and friends were incredible. I had a constant flow of encouraging emails and cards. Sometimes you don't realize all the connections you've made in your life until you reach out and ask for help. It was a stunning reminder that, in every interaction with another person, you have an impact, positive or negative. Later in life, the outcome of that impact will reveal itself to you.

September came, and I resolved that, whatever was about to happen, I was as prepared as I could be. I was no longer crying. Instead I was thinking that, whatever God had planned for me, I would follow.

The night before my surgery, I tucked each of my kids in like I did every other night. Since they were so young, we still did not use the word *cancer*. I didn't know if that was the right or wrong thing to do, but there's no rule book when it comes to being a sick mom. I told my oldest, who was deemed Mr. Responsible, that I would be gone in the morning and that Grandma would be there to help them get ready for school. My middle daughter, Miss Stubborn, kept a straight face and just nodded but later had an excruciating stomachache that made her cry a howling, painful cry for almost an hour straight as I held her tight. My youngest, Mr. Happy-Go-Lucky, was only six. And after I'd told him I had to go back to the hospital the next day, he simply asked, "Is this the time you're going to die?"

Hugging the kids the night before my surgery tore my heart out. No matter what you tell or don't tell your kids, they know. They hear the soft whispers around them. They see your expressions and your tears. They each own a part of your heart. *They know.*

~

Lip Tip: A little gloss never hurts. Lips look better moisturized than dry.

10

Hope Again

The surgery was a success. It only took a couple of hours, but when I woke up in the recovery room, I could immediately hear my voice. Relief, joy, all of it ran through every vein of my body. I wanted to jump up and dance. The surgeon told me he'd been able to get all the cancer and that I was done. And best of all, I didn't need any treatment. I was discharged from the hospital a few hours after the surgery and was home that night to tuck my kids in, never missing a beat.

I was feeling great, despite a little soreness. I was even talking already, a little weak, but I did not lose my voice this time. The cancer had returned, but I'd beat it—again. No one could wipe the smile off my face. I tried not to rush my recovery, but I had so much energy and joy from beating cancer a second time that I couldn't sit still. I was beyond ecstatic to have my voice, and I was eager to see if I could sing again.

Since this was my second time facing cancer and the second time I had a weakened voice, I started thinking more about the voice. Speaking, along with other senses, is something we easily take for granted. And it got me thinking about the power of "voice."

You need to use your voice wisely. Speak up for what you believe in. Use your voice to speak up for others who can't speak for themselves.

Use your voice to tell others how much you care and love them.

Use your voice to encourage and cry with those who need it.

Use it to sing silly songs to your kids.

Use your voice to praise God, who gave it to you.

Words are powerful; they come from the heart.

Don't miss the opportunities to share your heart; they may not come again.

Don't hesitate to say, "I love you," to those you love. Say it freely; say it often.

~

Lipstick: *Red*. Fiery, fierce. I was wearing red lipstick all the time. Red looks great on everyone; just be sure to keep the rest of your face neutral. There are red-blues, red-browns, and red-oranges. Wear when feeling inspired.

~

By October, one month after the surgery, I was back in vocal rehab practicing my speaking voice *and* my singing voice. My voice teacher, Marie, said I sounded better than ever. By

November, I was singing publicly once again. I felt amazing. I even signed up to do a half marathon because I was going to take control of my body. I was training my voice, my breathing, and my body. I felt a burning desire in my heart that God wanted me to somehow use this "gift" of cancer and life—not just my voice but my story. I just didn't know in what capacity.

Devastated

On December 17, three months after my surgery, I had a follow-up ultrasound with the same doctor who had done my last follow-up ultrasound and found the tumor; it was déjà vu.

"What did the surgeon tell you about your last surgery?" the doctor asked with furrowed eyebrows.

"He got it all," I replied.

"All of what?" He genuinely looked puzzled.

"He got all the cancer. He took it all out."

"He said that?"

"Yes. He said I was done with cancer. Why?" Now I was a little worried.

"Because there's still something there."

There's still something there. I hate those words

"What? Scar tissue maybe?" I said. I was trying not to panic as I lay there on the table, yet my voice was slightly higher.

"I don't think so. The ultrasound looks the same as last August, but the tumor is bigger."

Up until this point, I had never asked, Why me? I figured, Why not me?

But when the doctor said that there was still something there, I was stunned and sad, and I finally asked God *why*. I had three young kids at home. For the past three years, they'd had to navigate cancer with me, and I could not stand it. I was angry and dumbfounded. I did not know what to do. I wanted to understand, *Why me*? Why? I couldn't be logical anymore because nothing made sense.

"What's next?"

"Another PET scan."

I got dressed and left. No tears, just numb. The world moved in slow motion. I didn't talk to anyone. I didn't want to. I just drove around in silence.

Life is made of adversity, and how we choose to tackle it makes us who we are. I knew I would pull it together, but I didn't know how yet.

My PET scan was scheduled for December 24 at 6:00 a.m. Christmas Eve.

~

Lipstick: *Mauve-pinky / brown*. Easy. Anything with a brown undertone will mute the dominating color. If you're scared to go real pink, go with pinkish-brown; scared of bright red, try reddish-brown; and so on.

~

The morning of the twenty-fourth was surreal. I was in good spirits and ready to do what I needed to do. My close friends Lisa, Lissa, and Jen left their families at home Christmas Eve morning and came with me, at the crack of dawn, to the hospital for my PET scan. The staff had never seen so much support that early in the morning. I think sometimes you feel like you have to handle things on your own. But I quickly learned the importance of support; it's great for you and it's great for them.

After the three-hour process, the techs would not give me any information, despite my begging. They also said that, since it was a holiday and a Thursday, I might not get my results until Monday. It was torture, but I had no control. Me and my girlfriends went to breakfast, and thanks to all the laughter and chatter, I felt the most normal I had felt in a while.

Around four o'clock, as my family was getting ready for church, my cell phone rang. It was my doctor. My kids were sitting on my bed when I took the call.

"I have bad news."

My kids were silently listening because they knew I had gotten a PET scan that morning. I could not stop the tears as I walked into my closet, shut the door, and rolled myself into the fetal position on the floor. I don't know how long I was curled up and crying, but my husband came in and scooped me out of there telling me, "One day at a time." And it was Christmas.

I swiped on some red lipstick and sent a text to my friends. "The cancer is back."

Church was a blur, or maybe the tears in my eyes blurred my vision. I knew I had to tell my parents, but it was hard. I sat

67

next to my mom, and as the opening Christmas song started, I leaned over and whispered in her ear. I told her I had cancer again. I was hoping that, since we were in a public place, there would be no breakdown, but I was wrong. We both cried for the entire Christmas service.

At this moment in time, I felt defeated. My heart felt shattered into a million pieces. I was tired of fighting with my body. I'd tried eating better, exercising more, sleeping more, but here it was again. I was writing in my journal all the things I was grateful for, and there were so many things—people, friends, and doctors—but at that moment the sadness and fear took over. I was mentally and physically exhausted from fighting this giant battle with my body for two years.

After my holiday pity party, I buckled down and put my fighting gloves on. For the next few weeks, I prayed that God would lead me to the right surgeon and that I would make the right decisions about my cancer care. My doctor told me that the last surgeon didn't want to see me again because he refused to believe he'd missed taking out the large and growing tumor in my neck and thought it was just scar tissue. How confusing and lost that made me feel. My vocal doctor, Dr. Rubin, helped me by calling and referring me to a colleague at the institution where he had done his residency. That simple phone call brought me to the brilliant surgeon who did my third surgery.

~

Lipstick: *Nutty, Brazil nut, nut brown.* I found a lipstick named "Nutty" at a drug store. I *had* to get it because it was exactly how

I was feeling. All these colors are in the medium brown range and border a nude lip. Try to add a little extra color to your cheeks so people know you're alive and not a piece of cardboard.

~

I walked around in a daze during the time between my PET scan and my third surgery. I don't exactly know how I functioned as a mom, at work, with friends, and so on. I think I blocked parts of that time out of my mind. I was asked to sing a couple of times, to which I said yes. But after each time, I cried. I loved singing so much, and the thought of losing my voice for good broke my heart. I continued to train for the half marathon I'd registered for, fully knowing I would not be able to actually be in it. I would have breakdowns and cry at unexpected moments, even while running on a treadmill.

Shopping for lipstick helped, and in my quest for a sunny disposition, I bought my first ever orange lipstick. I am such a sucker. The more I tried to bring normalcy into my life, the harder it was. I felt like I was cracking.

I wasn't hearing from God much during this time because I was trying too hard to take care of things myself. I wasn't stopping long enough to sit and listen. I stayed overly busy and was trying desperately to stay "up," while being scared and wanting to just give up at the same time. I couldn't understand why God would give me my voice back twice, only to take it away in the end.

My husband was angry. And for the first time since I'd been diagnosed with cancer, I saw worry in his eyes. It was strangely refreshing. I was a complete wreck, my mom was a mess, my mother-in-law was a mess, and my kids tried really hard not to seem worried. But then my twelve-year-old asked if we should start learning sign language in case I couldn't talk anymore, which silenced my nine-year-old.

I lost it. I could not erase from my mind their faces the night before each of my surgeries as we prayed. That was the toughest time.

> Dear Cancer,
>
> I want to break up. It's not me; it's you. You keep wanting to get back together, and for whatever reason, my body lets you. Well, I'm done. I'm sick of all the game playing, and I'm sick of you messing with my mind. I wish I could say that my relationship with you has made me stronger, braver, more courageous, but I just don't know anymore.
>
> Now that you're trying to get back together, only bad feelings come up. You have made me more insecure about myself, you've made me sad, and I have shed too many tears over you. You not only affect me; you have widespread effects on the people I love and care about. They don't even know what to say anymore. You leave a train of destruction and pain everywhere you go. It may surprise you, but I love my life, and yes, thank you for opening my eyes and my heart constantly to

the blessings around me. Are you trying to teach me something? Is there a lesson to learn? Well, I got it. I'm good. So please stop showing up. Don't underestimate me. I am not going down.

Here we are at another crossroads. Will you ever leave me alone? Hate is a strong word that I never use, but I'm beginning to hate you. You have broken my heart over and over, but I will not let you break my spirit.

Anna

~

Lipstick: *Orange, coral.* This color is a little scary at first but actually looks *great* on everyone, especially in the summer. Be sure to wear minimal makeup if you're going to wear this bright and beautiful color.

12

Third Time's the Charm

I had mixed feelings the morning of my third surgery. Since the surgery was scheduled midmorning, I was able to take the kids to the bus stop for school. I was sad at the thought of what life would be like when they got to see me next, but I couldn't let that deter me. The risks for going back into my neck a third time were high. I could lose my voice completely. I could need a tracheostomy for the rest of my life. It didn't matter. The cancer had to come out.

My parents drove me to the hospital that morning because my husband was busy with work. Waiting at the hospital were my friends; my former boss; and, surprisingly, my father-in-law, who had driven over two hundred miles from Indiana. I felt loved and supported and my mind was at peace. I thought I'd be crying more, but I think I'd cried so much beforehand that I was just ready to get it over with.

Just before I was rolled into surgery, my husband showed up to meet my surgeon for the first time. They shook hands. He said, "Take care of my wife." Then he leaned down and kissed me on the forehead, and I was out.

I woke up from the four-hour surgery to find no one around me. I think it may have been a shift change for the nurses. Or maybe I woke up before they thought I would. I was in a daze, but knew I was not in a recovery room. I was already in a private hospital room. I could hear every beep and pulse of the machines that were still attached to me. I tried to hum, and I heard my voice, so I knew I still had it. I'm not sure how much time lapsed before the nurses started filtering in. They told me my surgery had gone amazingly well and that I would not need a tracheostomy. I couldn't speak loudly at the time. But at the very least, I knew I would have my voice back.

Life is precious and breathing really is a miracle, isn't it?

Two weeks after surgery, I was being fitted for my radiation mask. The doctors decided on seven weeks of external beam radiation to kill whatever was left in my neck. Being fitted for a mask is no party, especially if you're claustrophobic in any way. A mold was made for my head and upper chest, and they used that to create a mask that would fit tightly. This mask was then used to keep me completely still during my twenty-five-minute radiation sessions. Here's the other thing. The outer portion of the mask had snaps, which were used to bolt me down to the table. *Not cool.* Did I mention that this mask fit so tightly to my face that, after a single treatment, my face looked like it had gone through a waffle press?

For the next seven weeks (thirty-three treatments), I was driving myself over an hour from my house, five days a week, to get external beam radiation. Around week six, my parents had to take me because I was too weak to drive. No one told me that radiation would be so hard, and just being fitted for my mask nearly pushed me over the edge. I had never experienced a panic attack before, but I'm pretty sure that is what happened when they bolted me to the table the first time. There were eye holes and a hole for my mouth. *But why bother with eye holes?* Nobody wants to stare at the beams of radiation aimed at the neck coming from a large metal machine six inches away from the face. *No.*

After a surgery, you generally start feeling better over the following days, weeks, and months. With each passing week of radiation, you feel worse and worse. Your skin starts to burn. But by the time that happens, it usually means your insides are already burned. This is because, with radiation, you are actually burning from the inside out. With head and neck radiation, not only is your neck burning, but so are your tongue and your throat. I couldn't eat. I could barely swallow. And worst of all, the things I could swallow, I couldn't even taste.

As radiation progressed, the skin around my neck and my face got really dark, almost like I had been on vacation. My trips to the cosmetic counters were becoming more frequent because I was feeling so bad. My new skin color and swirl of emotions pushed me to try and buy new lip colors. I started buying lighter pinks and shimmery glosses. The one thing the radiation techs could see through my mask was my lip colors.

Halfway through my thirty-three treatments, my doctor asked if I could still sing for World Voice Day again, and I said yes. The pain in my throat was sometimes unbearable, but I knew it was short term. My dog was constantly licking my neck. I couldn't help but wonder if it was because she knew I was sick or if somehow my neck smelled like fried chicken.

The morning of World Voice Day, after seventeen radiation treatments, I started losing my voice, and breathing was becoming more difficult. It's funny how things happen overnight, in the blink of an eye. It turned out scar tissue was forming in my neck from the radiation. I decided to proceed with Voice Day anyway. The night was magical. I spoke, I cried, and I sang with what voice I had left. I felt inspired and hopeful by night's end.

I had about two weeks remaining of radiation when breathing got really difficult. I had gotten used to the routine of lying on the table and being bolted down, but now I couldn't lie down without having difficulty breathing. I had lost about thirty pounds, so my mask was a little loose as well. At this point, my radiation oncologist decided to scope my throat, and what he saw made him panic. My left functioning vocal cord was starting to slow down and move into my paralyzed right vocal cord. He wanted to do a tracheotomy right then and there and asked me to call my laryngologist for his recommendation.

The tears were back. I was losing my ability to breathe on my own. Dr Rubin, my laryngologist, confirmed what the radiation oncologist had seen. I begged him not to put a trach in, so he put me on high-dose steroids to help me finish out my radiation treatments. External beam radiation was by far the worst thing I had to endure. It was painful and draining and was an emotional roller coaster. I felt horrible, but the techs kept telling me how great I was doing and how wonderful I looked. I didn't envy their job, and I was grateful for them trying to keep my spirits up, but it was *hard*.

～

Lipstick: *Raisin*. Raisin is my favorite lipstick color from my all-around favorite cosmetic line. It is a deep plum color, and I chose it because I was being fried and pruned by the radiation. A raisin is a dried-up grape, and I felt like I was shriveling up into nothing.

～

After almost seven weeks of external beam radiation, I was done. Physically, I felt my absolute worst, but mentally, I was ecstatic. I had made it, and I felt done—not just done with radiation, done with cancer. On the last day, I received a congratulatory certificate and a lot of hugs, I got to ring the bell, and I got to take home my scary-looking mask. I'd lost almost forty pounds and couldn't eat, but I was finally on the long road to recovery.

Something most noncancer patients wouldn't know is that, when a patient goes through radiation, that patient has to have the treatment at around the same time every day to keep the level of radiation consistent. We (patients) see the same people every day based on our schedule. In the waiting room, while we wait our turn to be radiated, we get to know each other and learn each other's stories. That's how I met Bob.

Bob showed up in the radiation waiting room a few days

after I started. He was an older gentleman with gray hair and a gray moustache, the kind that curled up on the ends. His radiation time was immediately after mine. He was a Vietnam vet, married, and had kids and grandkids. We had the same exact cancer and the same time frame. He had a trach. He told me one of his dreams was to return to Disney. We kept each other company and swapped treatment stories and doctor stories. Bob became my security blanket and encouragement for each treatment. He was the angel God gave me for this time.

Every day, I would go in for my treatment before him and look over my shoulder, back at Bob. He always had a smile on his face and a thumbs-up. He helped me realize my strength. Bob and I finished radiation the very same day, and since I was first, I got to ring the bell first. He and his wife were amazing, and I loved him.

Bob and I continued to keep in touch over the years that followed. A few years after that last radiation treatment, though, I got a heart-shattering email:

> Anna,
>
> Looks like this will probably be it, my dear sweet Anna. Cancer is eating through my windpipe from both ends and is wrapped around my carotid artery, thus inoperable … Goodbye, my friend. Never give up! Am getting weaker every day. Keep up the faith, my sweet Anna, and I will always remember that genuine smile of yours over

your shoulder in the radiation oncology hallway. See you on the other side.

Love ya,

Bob

I felt broken. Bob passed away four years after I met him. He died on his birthday. He never made it back to Disney.

All it takes is eye contact. A smile can work miracles. So can holding someone's hand or giving him or her a hug. The whole time I was struggling to find God during this third episode with cancer, He was right in front of my face. He was in the hands and feet of my friends, family, and strangers who loved me and encouraged me. And He was in Bob, who, despite having the same struggles, moved beyond his pain to encourage me. God was everywhere, and He had been holding my hand this whole entire time.

Three months after finishing radiation and leaving the hospital, I had a PET scan. Three years, three surgeries, three positive PET scans, three surgeons, and three different hospitals. I *was done*. It was a clean PET scan, and I was finally, once again, deemed cancer free. When I got the news from my doctor, I sobbed.

When you've struggled with cancer so many times, joy doesn't come easily. I was happy but cautious. I paid close attention to any change in my body. Ask any cancer survivor, and I'm sure they'll tell you the same thing. It was a much longer recovery than I'd anticipated, but I was hopeful, and the lipstick counters never failed to put a smile on my face.

Five months after radiation, my vocal coach told me I'd be able to sing again, but it would be a little different. I felt part of a miracle, but the greater miracle was all the people who had stepped in and e-mailed, prayed, brought meals to my family, and encouraged me. I had gotten close to my lipstick counter girls—Catherine, Diane, Leslie, and Tanita. They called and checked on me and were always ready with colors for me to try, along with numerous samples. In the times I lost my voice, I learned to listen. And in that silence, I heard God the loudest.

Lipstick: *Red, siren*. Red, hot, beautiful, and bold. Ready to take on life.

13

You Have to Be Kidding

After battling and beating cancer the third time in 2010, life resumed as normal—well, as normal as it could be. My perspective on life and living had changed significantly. *How could it not?* I went back to work, the kids returned to being kids with a healthy mom. I wasn't really singing much anymore because the scar tissue in my neck, along with a paralyzed vocal cord, really took its toll. But I had learned to be okay with that (most of the time). I took more risks, and I looked for the magic in the moments. I realized I had been given the gift of living, and I thought about how I wanted to live.

Cancer opened my eyes to life, and I guess it made me a little more selfish. I was more selfish with my time and how I spent it. I said yes more, and I tried to be more fearless. After cancer, I got to take a long view of my life, like an out-of-body experience, and I assessed everything. I was unbelievably grateful for life and the people that surrounded me. In the few years after battling cancer three times, my marriage ended in divorce. You could say it was selfish, but it was actually one of the healthiest decisions I've made for myself, ever.

Life moved forward, and a couple years after the divorce, I met an amazing man. He attended my church, and we had a few mutual friends, so I knew he was "safe." After our first meeting, I felt my heart exhale. After our first date, I felt like I was home. In my mind, I thought, *There you are.* Five years after my cancer nightmare and divorce, with more clarity and perspective, I married Jim, and I couldn't be happier.

With large doses of radiation, there is still a risk of damage to some of the nerves surrounding the cancer they're trying to kill (among other things). I was told that I could have side effects for the next ten years. So, at year seven post-radiation, when my fingers and arm were becoming numb, I blew it off as a side effect (neuropathy is a typical side effect of radiation). It had been a few years since seeing my laryngologist, so I made an appointment for a checkup of my vocal cords. No surprise, my right vocal cord was still paralyzed, and my left was thankfully "doing the work."

"Everything looks good. Is there anything else? Anything change?" he asked.

"Not really. I can't feel the fingertips of my left hand, and my left arm, in general, is weaker. But that's to be expected," I responded matter-of-factly.

"Has it been getting worse?" he asked with a touch of concern now in his voice.

"Yes, just over the past year."

"Hmm, I'm not really comfortable with that. When was your last PET scan?" Now he was writing notes.

"Not sure, maybe three or four years ago?"

"Okay. I'm going to contact your other doctor and recommend a CT scan just to make sure."

Off to a routine CT scan I went, with no expectations of anything.

A day after my CT scan, it was a Tuesday in July, the sun was already out, and the air was warm. The kids were still sleeping. But my husband, Jim, was at the ice rink playing in his early-morning hockey league. While in bed, sun beaming through the slats of the blinds in our bedroom, I reached over, grabbed my phone, and decided to open the patient portal to see if there were any results from the CT:

> Impressions: Several lung nodules in left and right lobe measuring … with the largest in the left upper lobe measuring 9mm … Worrisome of metastatic cancer.

My pulse raced, my hands shook, and I felt like I was being sucked into the earth. All at once, my world felt like it was caving in, and I felt very alone. In July 2017—seven years and two months after my last radiation treatment—I was diagnosed with Stage IV cancer, with distant metastasis to my lungs. My cancer was back with a vengeance.

Lipstick: *Nude* (again). During this period, I was depressed and sad and therefore wanted to disappear. Nude lippie it was.

~

The year following this diagnosis was by far one of the most difficult years of my life. I had so many questions. Fear took hold of me, but depression and sadness took a stronger hold. Again, I plodded along each day, working full-time, taking care of the kids, and crying in the car or in my bedroom at night.

Just about every doctor told me, "Don't look at the statistics because every person is different." Something every patient will tell you (because Google is now a standard), "Doesn't matter what they say. I'm looking."

The statistics on Stage IV metastatic thyroid cancer with distant metastasis are not good—50 percent gone in five years, 90 percent in ten years. So ten years if I'm lucky.

I thought about my kids and how much I'd be missing—weddings, grandkids, and even high school graduation. For the last ten years, my young children, now becoming young adults, have had a mom dealing with cancer. On top of that, their parents went through a divorce. How would all of this craziness affect them? It was too much.

My oldest was in college already, but my daughter wasn't yet a senior in high school, and my youngest son was still in middle school. *Will I be around when he graduates high school?* Every single moment with them was precious and heartbreaking. I burst into tears with every hug and even every look. I clung to each moment like I was hanging on for dear life. At this point, my thoughts were focused on being alive for my youngest son's high school graduation. Four years. *Will I be there for him in four years?* He would be eighteen by then. *Will I be there to usher him into adulthood?* These were, by far, the saddest days.

Then there was Jim. I had left a difficult marriage and had found the man of my dreams. And now this? I'd met a man who treated me like a queen, who made me laugh and filled my life with joy. He was loving and kind and funny, my breath of fresh air for this second half of life. He brought his two kids into our marriage, making us a family of seven. I kept asking myself, but really asking God, *Why can't things just be good for a while?*

I had a hard time telling friends that the cancer was back. I almost didn't want to say it because I thought people would roll their eyes and think, *Geez. Again?* I didn't want to ask for prayer yet again. Anytime I would say the words, I'd start crying. I tried to remain strong, but the way people would look at me with sadness or maybe pity broke me. I didn't know what to do with myself. Every single day I felt like I was moving in slow motion again as life rushed by.

14

What Now?

Time is precious. When you get a Stage IV diagnosis, you know your life is all about *time*. You are a walking time bomb, and you don't know when the timer will go off. Historically, there has been no cure for Stage IV cancer, just medicines to help prolong the time you have left (although with advances in medicine, there are more and more cures being discovered). I kept wondering, *What am I doing with my life? What do I want to do in the time I have left, whether it's one year or another fifty?* At this point, every moment mattered.

In the midst of getting scans and blood work every three months to measure my tumors, I assessed my life and came up with a dream for the rest of it. After years of buying and writing about lipstick, I decided that I wanted to start my own lipstick company. I also wanted to help other cancer fighters somehow. So I decided partial proceeds were going to be given to some of the smaller, grassroots organizations I knew of and had been a part of. I wanted to somehow give back physically too, to volunteer at events, sit with other cancer fighters, and do whatever was needed to shout to the world that *no one fights alone.* Cancer fighters can help other fighters. I wanted to scream, "We are in it together."

This was a crazy dream.

I didn't know anything about running a business or the lipstick/cosmetic industry except for which brands were my favorite. I knew I didn't want the lipsticks my company offered to have all the toxic chemicals normally found in lipstick (although there have been significant strides to change that in mainstream makeup). I wanted it to be moisturizing so that, even women going through treatment with dry lips, could wear it and be comfortable. I wanted it to feel good and to look good.

I went back to Google, and instead of looking at statistics and research related to my cancer, I looked up how to make lipstick in my kitchen. I researched ingredients and brands that were committed to "clean" makeup. I researched antiaging ingredients and moisturizing ingredients and finally decided that I needed to find a cosmetic chemist.

When I told my husband about my crazy dream, he looked at me funny. I had Stage IV cancer, and we had five teenagers, with one in college and four more to go. It was not an ideal time to start a business. He asked me hard questions. How much would this dream cost? With the millions of lipsticks out there, how would mine be different? I had no answers, just my vision and mission of what I wanted it to be.

In the end, he said, "Whatever you need, I'll support you."

Note to all of you singles out there—find someone who loves and supports you this much.

I'm not sure if he thought I would keep pursuing the dream or not. After about a week of researching companies, ingredients, and so on, I showed him my notebook with all the people I had spoken to and all the prices on development and manufacturing I'd received. At that point, he knew I was serious. Immediately, he came up with the bare bones of a business plan, and he tutored me on owning a business, since he had owned his own businesses in the past. That's when I knew he was really "in" on my dream as well, and I think this was the moment my mental healing began.

I launched my lipstick company, The Lipstick Journey, in December 2018, seventeen months after being diagnosed with Stage IV cancer. It has been a wild ride, but it has given me new life. Until recently, I was still getting scanned every three months. But since the diagnosis, the tumors have been stable, so the scans have now moved to every six months. The word *stable* has become one of my favorites. Stable to a Stage IV cancer fighter means that the cancer is still there, but it's either slow growing or not growing. Perfect.

My faith is still my anchor. It has always been strong, but with all that has happened, it has evolved to something deeper. I have learned so much about faith and what it really meant to have hope. God was everywhere, in nature and in people. The love and kindness of family, friends, and strangers showed the loving realness of God. All of their prayers and words of encouragement were balm to my soul. The death and rebirth of flowers in spring showed the beautiful creation and plan of God. I learned that hope was active and it was simply taking another step forward, with gratitude, believing that there would be something else to be grateful for the next day. My faith, which had become deeper but simpler, and the goodness I saw in people gave me hope that continues today.

My youngest son is going to be a junior in high school, so seeing him graduate is on the horizon. I don't sing anymore, but cancer has given way to new dreams, like my lipstick company. It is never too late to dream. Jim and I talk of retirement every now and then, but my mindset is still focused on living day-to-day. I have a very keen awareness of time and living in the absolute present. I don't want to miss the magic, and there is always magic. In my darkest moments, there was—and still is—love.

Dear Anna,

You have been in a long battle with cancer, not once, but four times, beginning right at the prime of your life—good career, young mom. You thought that music and being a singer defined your identity, or at least your public persona, but now you know better. When you got cancer the first time and it took your vocal cord, you thought you'd lost your voice. Today, your "voice" is even stronger. You may not be able to sing, but you finally found the strength in your own inner voice. It took a lot to find it, but it's here.

You have doubted your strength and your ability to push through and it's okay. You are strong. Always remember what you've been through. It's also okay to feel week, anxious, sad, and afraid. And if you have to use the "cancer card," do it. You will have moments of joy and laughter. Soak those in. Reach out to your friends and family and don't be afraid to ask for help, ask for hugs, and ask for prayers. Cry your eyes out. Find solitude when you need to. Say yes more, but also say no and mean it.

Lastly, don't lose hope. Enjoy every moment and find the magic. Never forget that God loves you and He's been with you, holding your hand every step of the way. Think of all the blessings that this journey has given you and all the people who have surrounded you with love and support along the way. Keep loving, keep living, and keep dreaming big dreams.

Love,

Me

The Lipstick Journey Lipstick (in Order of Top to Bottom on Cover)

Stormy. A deep, dark plum. There are days when the sun doesn't shine. We go through storms in our lives that many times are not in our control. Wear this color on those dark days, knowing that there is *still* color to the day. Although the days are dark, a little color reminds us that all people, like all days, are colorful. *Be courageous.*

Serene. A medium brown color with an undertone of peach. This wonderful neutral is what to wear when you're at peace with just being you. Sometimes there are days when not a lot of color is necessary. This neutral and wearable everyday color will let the life in your eyes shine through. *Be grateful.*

Fierce. A neutral, deep red. This is the color you want to wear when you know that you are enough. You can take on life with strength and confidence, no matter what obstacle or trial you face. You are fierce. You are strong. You are enough. *Be free.*

Playful. A brighter plum-raspberry. This color is pure fun! Wear this color when you want to put extra life into your day. Wear it on the sunny days or on the rainy days—any time you feel confident, thankful, and just full of joy. Playful is what you want to be. Bright enough to light up your face, yet suitable for every skin tone. *Be yourself.*

Promise. A sheer pink with a hint of peach and a little shimmer. Wear this color to remind yourself that tomorrow is a new day. It's a color full of hope and promise, and it's a "pinky promise" to yourself to be gentle to you. Wear this color alone or on top of your favorite color to add a little shimmer and to hold onto the hope and promise of a new day. *Be at peace.*

Life is your canvas.